Dr Mia Morgan White

THESE ARE YOUR ANCESTORS

APEX TELEVISION NETWORK

I still Love you, Mia

LIBRARY OF CONGRESS NUMBER: *2024941163*

Belle Lumiere Belle Media TRUE NEWS INTERNATIONAL **ISBN:** 9781603619103

Author : **Dr Mia Morgan White**

: **Mia Morgan White**

Contact information:

mailing address One Embarcadero Center

#2271 San Francisco California and by e-mail WilhelminaPureGood@gmail.com

Electronic Book ISBN: 9781603618106

Paperback **ISBN:** 9781603619103

Copyright NOTICE: ©2024 Belle Lumiere ® Dr Mia Morgan White

Additional Copyrights concepts and lectures / courses years listed multiple editions:

©2024, ©2000, ©2003, ©2018, ©2020 Belle Lumiere ® All rights reserved.

No part of this publication may be reproduced, distributed, or transmitted in any form or by any means, including photocopying, recording, or other electronic or mechanical methods, without the prior written permission of the publisher, except in the case of brief quotations embodied in critical reviews and certain other noncommercial uses permitted by copyright law. For permission requests, contact

GoldenArigatoGroup@Gmail.com

"Although the author and publisher have made every effort to ensure that the information in this book was correct at press time, the author and publisher do not assume and hereby disclaim any liability to any party for any loss, damage, or disruption caused by errors or omissions, whether such errors or omissions result from negligence, accident, or any other cause."

This Book is about the Brain Beauty and Wellness, medical, fitness or similar content: "This book is not intended as a substitute for the western medical advice of physicians. The reader should regularly consult a physician in matters relating to his/her biological health and particularly with respect to any symptoms that may require diagnosis or medical attention."

These ARE Your ANCESTORS

dR Mia Morgan White

Paperback ISBN : 9781603619103
Electronic Books ISBN: 9781603618106

Soul

The other day someone called Dr. Morgan "Monkey" for the 1122 time since she moved back to San Francisco WHEREAS, the Consultant Dr. Mia Morgan White offers consulting services and a Black Certified Mensa Genius and a "99.999999 %" IQ rarity owned Think Tank called OMEGA, in the field of the Human Brain, Product Development and IT, like Keiretsu Capital Partners.

Wellness and Spiritual Histories and Protection for Mind Body Soul for all races, creed and species on the Planet Earth and Cosmos History. Practices 24 years in Western Neuroscience since her awarding for her thesis in 2000 and Eastern Medicine since her studies insights and senior project in 1997 for certification was turned into a textbook for the school from which she graduated that students have been required to read for 4 of their classes for graduation requirements 18 years.

Her services of the Consultant to render consulting services with regard to Scope of consulting services has become unlimited. Her services and remote viewing have become available to the public and private sectors for the first time in 28 years.

NOW, THEREFORE, This book is for everyone in OUR GREAT COUNTRY TO BE USED ALL AROUND the Planet To Make Our Lives Happier and Easier.

1. Term

Every cycle of sickness, illness, disease and affliction from the evil powers of my father's & mothers house, break!

In the name of Jesus. 🙏

Everybody needs to focus on love . It's not about race in a lot of racist witches and satanist, luciferians have been attacking with spells and Chinese black magic old literature would call Demons attack (Donte, Doone, Picasso, Shakespeare) Know attacking me and Blacks people out of part of their redlining and dragging down of Black Peoples. So there's a lot of death and financial attacks on Chosen Ones who are trying to protect Black Men and girls our children before they lose their rights and Souls.

2. Consulting Services

When someone guesses your vocabulary and the vocabulary they lie and say you used; is based on a stereotype for your race class or gender, but you don't fit the stereotype of such the words

it's because the stereotype was already in their head and when they lie, they applied **the lie**/it to you so BuT THE LIE IS VOCABULARY and YOU wouldn't Use. Meaning the words not YOUR syntax or verbiage. Don't believe lies about your ancestors HERE THEY ARE.
Sometimes we can look at it STEREOTYPES WITHIN STEREOTYPES. Those people who are using other people THEY would HOPE apply stereotypical behavior to you certain social classes with/would call set up or some slang including y'all and always but we need to remember it's NEVER all of anybody. They were recruiting Flying Monkeys HARMING THEIR SOULS AND YOURS.

But there is 8000 years YEP EIGHT THOUSAND YEARS of certain frequency and LOWER vibrations no matter what body it's in having PATTERN behaviors to cause discord or lower the vibrational frequency away from God and love.

3. Compensation

Bad deals were made So the KJV Bible was not written to fool you it was to show you God's Resume Source Universes Resume. AND WHAT BAD DEALS LOOK LIKE. How they were made and how to break them Get out of them.

4. Intellectual Property Rights in Work Product

The Parties acknowledge and agree that The Ancestors you were told were your ancestors ARE IN SCIENTIFIC FACT THE WORLD'S ANCESTORS

5. Confidentiality

Simple your ancestors are also the people who are ones who survived without making deals with their Souls. Everyone else has interim ancestor stories not you because the beings wanted you not to continue to be the peoples who were still not making deals for favor. Realize what your World Ancestors realized MILLIONS of years AGO deals were not necessary. So true history was hidden to keep you from your Divinity.

6. Noncompetition

New TESTAMENT and WORKS FROM 800 Cultures honor the term of this Agreement and for Millions of months daily actions thereafter, the bodies given the gift of life shall not engage, directly or indirectly, as an employee, officer, manager, partner, manager, consultant, agent, owner or in any other capacity, in any gateopening that caused the dark ages with the Christ light fixing it and giving us the answer key. So it was your ancestors and their friends, some faithful to light of every culture race and vibration REALIZED FROM A BOOK THEY READ daily or weekly LOVE IS THE HIGHEST VIBRATIONAL FREQUENCY. (SCIENCE) CHI GONG HEALS WITH THAT FREQUENCY and all emotions of that frequency to example that which Jesus showed us Cleans and Heals ask and hurt child whose Mom kisses their boo. It heals removes the pain. JUST LIKE DARK CHI does the opposite.

7. Nonsolicitation of Customers

DARK CHI DOES NOT HAVE A GET you to make an ADVERTISED DEAL IF you are tricked into willing unkindness. During the term of this Agreement that you didn't know you made with Evil the human in this book withstood those tricked and all the hate thrown at them. And THAT is how by the 1910 you had SOUL FOOD and for THE NEXT 80 YEARS EVERY SOUL ON THE PLANET CHOOSE darkness or light. [Number months only affected by if churches were tricked into tell some people those people were not welcome. SO AS THE ORIGINAL PEOPLE YOU KNEW BACK THEN IN YOUR DNA the outcome of A: DARK DEAL and B: JESUS DELIVERING THEM FROM THE DEMONS THAT RAN RAPID DURING AMERICAN SLAVERY. WHERE A LOSE OF INNOCENCE LEAD TO GOOD MEANING SOUTHERNERS not realizing the loss of soul by more than 60% of slave owners will not, directly or indirectly, solicit or attempt to solicit any evil business from any of the Companies clients, prospects, employees or contractors HAVE BEEN LONG FORGOTTEN for ALL RACES BACK THEN and the OTHER 1100 TIMES Slavery happened to every culture around the world, During American Slavery there WERE RICH BLACKS WHO OWNED POOR WHITE PEOPLE AS SLAVES. So from 1890 to 1976 Every American knew the choice was Good and Evil. WITH EVERY ACT even retaliation, I've seen what pure evil can do AND SO HAVE YOU, YOUR ANCESTORS HERE KNEW NOT TO GIVE UP THEIR SOUL'S LIGHT and NOT LEND THEIR BODY to Dark Chi. THEY WERE NOT STUPID OR WEAK. They knew the REAL GAME WAS TO STAY LIGHT.

8. Nonsolicitation of Employees

ABUSE OF POWER Therefore SYSTEMATIC, the PEOPLE will not, directly or indirectly, recruit, solicit, or induce, or attempt to recruit, solicit, or induce, any of the GAMES BY EVIL, IF THEY ARE TRICKED INTO seeing their corrupt (CORRUPT DOES NOT MEAN ILLEGAL IT BY DEFINITION MEANS EVIL)

CORRUPT MEANS BEING EVIL - under the influence of evil THAT is the definition of corruption in 88 countries except in America it was a campaign in the 1944 because AMERICA WAS NOT AS EASILY TRICKED.

BECAUSE OUR MASON FOUNDING FATHERS SPIRITUALLY PROTECTED OUR COUNTRY

HOW YOU MIGHT ASK (ANSWER CHECK YOUR MONEY) so we didn't openly get tricked.

tricks had to happen in the dark BECAUSE IN GOD WE TRUST. Dr Mia NEXT BOOK Indemnification

I'm not a strange adult. I'm a happy very comfortable STOIC adult. I was a strange child because my mother let me be - thank goodness. I will call my mother, master Yoda, which is true and to regards her quips and her knowledge of the world. She loved mythology. And so I would be at the ballet which to this day I only like the Russian ballet because you can't talk while attending any ballet. The Russian Ballet at the first arrondissement in Paris there is too many wonderful things to watch it is the one ballet where you are too amazed to want to talk. And what I liked to do since I was 3 years old is talk to my mom about the things I was learning or listen to her teaching me stuff.

Now I say so lovelying that woman never shut up, sometimes people think

I talk a lot but that's because they never met my mom. My mom taught me with her every breath if she wasn't saying how much she loved me she was teaching me something because of how much she loved me so at the symphony or the opera house where you can talk, you can whisper and you're not supposed to, but when you're little kid people understand, cut you a break. I would just say one word, I would be mesmerized. Classical Music It's my favorite thing in the world other than God and Shakespeare and they play the music and At my #4 thing Opera since I was 8. Tchaikovsky I would whisper to my mother at the theatre and then the next one I would as very quietly after squeezing her hand Chopin because I don't like Chopin as much as I like Wolfgang and Tchaikovsky, kinda like my favorite painters at the Renaissance and the masters so because of my mom who didn't teach my Love for Sarah Vaughn and Ella FitzGerald I learned that from my childhood obsession with black and white movies and of course techni-color musicals. I have spiritual gifts God sent me here that way. My Mom would let me stay up and watch them all night if I woke up after my proper bedtime. Me that most people don't know that stuff or people that look like me we weren't even wanted in those places she just took me everywhere she thought would give me a wonderful life.

I don't even know how she did it, but she did it, so you should be lucky to be as weird as me.

I was born with my spiritual gifts so she always supported that and I was born with a extremely high achieved genius IQ so she was always supportive of my gifts made sure I knew stick with God 100% all the way I still remember my first prayer God is love we'd have a lot less fighting if every religion no matter what they're calling God would say. God is love before they think before they speak before they act because vibrationally you if racist it doesn't matter if you go to church the devil owns you. You're his minion you little army made 1 billions of people thinking going to church and reading the Bible. You belong to God, but if you're racist, all those behaviors are demonic entitlement narcissist to Satan, which are still not as entertaining as the boys on Wall Street they are upper level demons. They have parties now if you go home early enough, the party course is a great party because you don't know what happens after so you never figure out their demons, but they know their demons. There's sniffing Coke naked people because sometimes the bad boys were hungry they started having Sushi on the people so they could just be wild and have drugs and snack off the people tables! but what we're all energetics or spiritual things things that was happening while we were there that we just didn't know because we didn't have those goggles!! so I would say make God your goggles because I had Clients and that world spent so many years protecting me because they knew I don't drink I don't smoke.

I say I didn't even curse. Until God made hipsters now I'll tell you something; My mom used to say she never cursed till we became teenagers, and I thought she was making a joke, but I think that she was just telling the truth because now I can pinpoint -I didn't curse for 40 years I mean, not counting little teen kid when you're trying to be a grown-up listening to like Richard Pryor that stuff will make you sneak and think being a grown up by cursing, but I always used to tell my students it just shows a lack of vocabulary.

Thank God, hipsters evil narcissist, cruel people sitting in the senior section watching seniors fall because the seniors are standing up or trying to stand up as a bus moves and they just sit there smiling like the evil thing that they are inside. I'm not picking on suicidal humans I'm picking the demons in those bodies, the transmuted them and you think they're just selfish young people, but cruelty to each other is the reason for the suicides we had to change we had to write a new law if you go on social media and encourage someone to commit suicide -who by the way making a live recording suicide to expose all the bullies and all the people who are in classrooms, pretending to be teachers because they didn't have teaching credentials. The kids haven't been learning, don't call them stupid they weren't being taught. They didn't have Miss Crabtree.

They had people with an agenda to transmute them into something Evil who had no teaching credentials so they spent six hours a day talking and gossiping about the opposite of what you were trying to raise them to be. This was not a mystery. School Districts did this on purpose.

They wanted to steal money from those who are already poor and kept down based on red lining and systemic issues and then it went right into the wealthy schools as well, so the transmutation was not an accident and now you can see evil for what it is, there are people who are brought up to be evil?

There are people who were born to be evil who decided said to themselves "now I don't wanna do that", even though you would say bloodline or species or cursed bloodline, or they are not doing anything, but loving the world and loving God and serving in every way they can.

Or you can be into changing the name of Jesus, but if you change it, change it to Christ, the Christ or Christos because that's what Evil calls him as they're running away because he's coming.

so what do you think it looks like? If you say his name a lot and keep him in your mind and your soul keep him in your heart. Keep him in Meridians or your soul, being, in your body. is the light that comes off of a lightbulb- painting a fine art museum that shows a halo or a gold glow around people just like it somebody's eyes that are completely flat dark or black it's showing you the type of soul, but that was a trick in the 70s for people to do drugs promiscuous be indiscriminate with their energy in their bodies by sharing it with other bodies that were unholy or dark or broken. abuse happens so evil can get into your body whether it's beat with a fist or otherwise whether it's verbal intrusion or unbelievable targeting kindness so God is love whatever you call God and yes, it is possible to change

Christo's name into other names and take on bigger demons so you can fight evil with a level of evil you control by saying this is what my ancient ancestors did. they forgot to tell you they tricked you to kill your brother and when you learn that was a game that locked up, they tricked you into taking on a bigger demon in order to fight them that you can control better and you control them better by consciously calling Source the phrase the most high God comes from you're saying not the gods not the mythology not the different pantheons of different cultures and different continents you're saying God, the source God and Jesus doesn't care if you show Christ Love and Christ does not come out your mouth.

They know the new testament see those are your ancestors of the Old Testament, but they are not your ancestors. They are the world's ancestors.

They are the ancestor of every race on the planet because that's how different races and species developed in a black body, your ancestors are the beautiful people that survived deities of slavery, red lining, prejudice, systemic racism, hatred, and any other trash demon that doesn't like their life thinking it means they can mistreat you and the police won't do anything and they think the law won't be very good but very good folks who would watch people being lynched at a picnic after being transmuted to lower vibration so call it lower vibration all kind of stuff. For me I say God Jesus light dark dark Demons light Chi I will call the Angels. And you're not supposed to be a jell-O mixture of it and you can transmute yourself but transmute you instantly. anyone who has been very dark or purely dark will tell you they transmuted by doing what different text of every culture tells you and by the way if you read them all of the new testament in ancient stuff, the old testament and ancient texts from every religion and every culture and every continent tell the same story, when I was a little kid, I told my mom that I think everybody loves Jesus and that just he appeared to them and looked like them so they will feel comfortable.

BUT when I grew up AND when you read them, the stories are the same every dimension every space every time every timeline, Christos shows up the same love strength and he's asking God everything Doing that Source tells him to do so the universe was made because God loves you you were made because God loves you and you can worship anything you want because you have free will and if you lose control of your mind or your body, you don't lose control of your soul. Your soul gets pushed out, when you get filled with darkness, all souls were made from Source.

You're all a piece of a star. You're all starlight... When stars have no light scientifically they're considered dead so maybe sometimes you act like a zombie, some people with energetic parasites you think they act like vampires, but if you ever seen a movie, Nosferatu are ugly so that's really what you're dealing with. You're not dealing with Vlad, you're not dealing with you're not dealing with a bloodline makes your mind think they're handsome. You're dealing with Nosferatu so ask God to remove everything not GOD.

Now ask God to show you true friends and stop being little grayscale minions if you're gonna make a deal least do it on purpose. Not tricked so if you use anger and something using you, it doesn't have to be some low level frequency using you- doesn't have to be low level demon or evil using you anger fear and doubt can be a upper level demon sitting in a room And laughing I have video. I'm gonna show you if you go to social media or Class/Course right. evil the room with anger to use other peoples bodies to harm ever other body. They couldn't touch some bodies because that body runs on Christ light and you can see the light body source and saying things you wouldn't expect them to say because they're saying what God is telling them to say, to protect them.

Whereas evil that they push in your space and then use it so you harm someone else or have you inflict pain on someone else the moment you feel better hurting someone else evil has you. that your sign that evil in your space when you feel better harming someone you are darkness. And not sexy darkness like my friend

Michael he's third generation darkness. He called that low budget magic and say don't act like that. At least you know I prefer my Evil in Armani doesn't mean Evil it was because so I didn't want to give any part of my being to be cruel to others so I decided to make a joke about Armani because you know they're in a suit and they are in complete control of their actions and deeds and a completely aware that they made a deal with Evil, don't let Evil make deals and I would highly recommend you not! that so the last story I'm gonna tell you here instead of in video with proof footage is if you change to a religion where you're still rejecting God you need to ask who you are excepting

or what you are accepting and it might be your bloodline so it might be normal for you not to be with God But a football field: it's a football field so you didn't change timelines. You didn't raise consciousness. You're not at Crown chakra you know "to use of a vacuolar" that some people might understand better you're not where your the top of your head is glowing cause so much light your body that little kids wave when you walk by and amazed to see you, nice clean soul. You just went from 10 yard line to the 40 yard line or the yard line to the 20 yard line on the same plane where dark Chi is comfortable.

It would you be gossiping soccer mom or a gossiping church mother have different low vibrations- the church mother has a Lower vibration and a gossiping soccer mom they both running, they're both harming souls, but one is sitting in a house where no matter what you've done no matter what you've been or what was done to you or how dark you got You are still welcome to come in that church house which transmute you only light and goodness. but when you gossiping at church and have your judgment at church when you're unkind at church, you are making the building less light.

the building and the group of people meeting transmute everyone who comes - while you're there after they leave and hopefully for a large part of their life. it's Enough to deal with whatever the world might be doing so that they would change consciousness then they can change timelines When they encounter less people that lower their vibration and then I know the ones right now they have the thought that the higher you get in your light, the more something dark tries to drag you back down if you go to the top of the religious pyramid and you and when I say religious pyramid,

I didn't make a mistake and using word pyramid is what God told me to say right now, Every single thing I've done that was I've done that since I was born, and my parents encouraged it that if you just say IS THIS God /not God, it takes care of homophobia God not God will you let God teach your kids. People were with no teaching credentials for 17 years now is 22 years but I saw you do it for 17 years Being place it and you're right to do whatever you want and to be racist and classist and sexist so the devil in his team and and you accepted them because you were too busy being his puppets in Corporate Office, in the boardroom, on the street walking not saying hi, on the bus, in your car running a stoplight, running a red light or speeding towards pedestrians every time you do something that's not love. It's not God and unless you come from a demonic bloodline, those are not your ancestors. These are your ancestors your ancestors choose not to make a deal with their soul to escape racism. These are your ancestors those who did not kill their brother and took a lot of crap* took a lot of hardship* took a lot of poverty* took a lot of suffering* took a lot of devastation* to not go to jail, not lose their soul *they saw life as a game that was being played so if you go from the 2 yard line where you obviously know you're doing Evil stuff to the 40 yard line where you doing selfish egotistical stuff especially being sexist or chauvinistic then you are messing with the creative counterpart that loves you. And cleans your soul on a daily basis just because she loves you Her love cleans so when you abuse that you have a sex demon as a mate you're getting abused and you don't even know it just getting darker, darker, darker and more polluted and more polluted. You think she's getting your demons you're getting her demons and every demon she slept with while you were at work, the bag or the bag or using phrases like the bag you know what the bag is your: body is the bag your body the bag your soul is that the more the bag the darker thing can come in and live there and shop that's why they can't cook be glad God make sure they couldn't cook because they're putting things in your food. Things unmentionable monthly things if you know what

I mean Vibes and physical things unmentionable monthly things or somebody else's unmentionable monthly things that's why you can't make away that's why you can't trust your friends that's why you live a certain lifestyle and you gonna be up going to who they use to set you up it's going to be your girl because she's a demon And if you are bad and horrible, and you are lucky to be blessed by God with a good girl, your entire community is going to do everything they can to destroy that relationship because they see that relationship transmuting it. They see it in lifetime live action lifetime right they see you changing God is changing you, because you're around her but what she doesn't know is darkness is also changing her and it's bringing people to her so you can stay the king of your little posse. Demon serve Demon pool water after the rain.

There's a lot of puddles each one is a type of person or a group of people so you can be in a lot of little puddles but that energy is feeding darkness. You think it's feeding you because you got as much lobster shrimp designer stuff as you want but what you don't have is why they gave you all that other stuff because since you got here, my brother, my sister is your light and your light keeps out the darkness.

Thanks For Watching   GOD IS LOVE

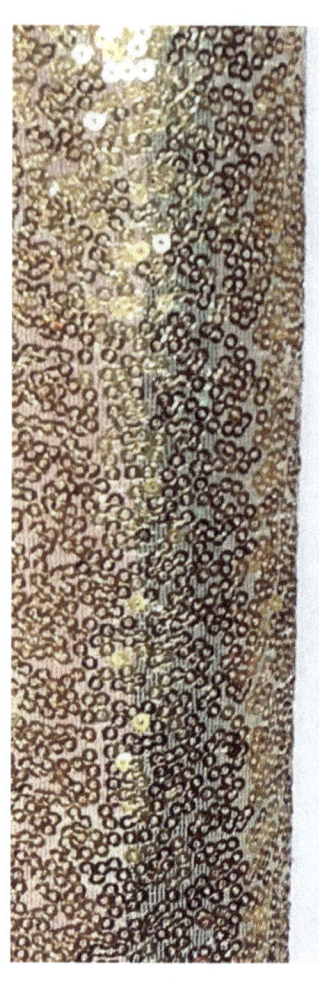

www.ingramcontent.com/pod-product-compliance
Lightning Source LLC
Chambersburg PA
CBHW081148230426
43664CB00018B/2853